95p

D1807847

Surinam

in pictures

VISUAL
GEOGRAPHY
SERIES

Surinam is aptly called "The Land of Sunny Faces" because of its successful melting-pot policy. Here girls representing the many races of Surinam proudly wear their own folk costumes: Chinese, Amerindian, Dutch, Lebanese, Hindu, Javanese, Bush Negro, and Creole.

Prepared by **MARTHA MURRAY SUMWALT**

 STERLING PUBLISHING CO., INC. NEW YORK

 Oak Tree Press Co., Ltd.
London & Sydney

VISUAL GEOGRAPHY SERIES

Afghanistan
Alaska
Argentina
Australia
Austria
Belgium and Luxembourg
Berlin—East and West
Brazil
Bulgaria
Canada
The Caribbean (English-
  Speaking Islands)
Ceylon
Chile
Colombia
Czechoslovakia
Denmark
Ecuador
England
Ethiopia
Finland
France
French Canada
Ghana
Greece
Guatemala

Hawaii
Holland
Honduras
Hong Kong
Hungary
Iceland
India
Indonesia
Iran
Iraq
Ireland
Islands of the
  Mediterranean
Israel
Italy
Jamaica
Japan
Kenya
Korea
Kuwait
Lebanon
Liberia
Malaysia and Singapore
Mexico
Morocco
New Zealand
Norway

Pakistan
Panama and the Canal
  Zone
Peru
The Philippines
Poland
Portugal
Puerto Rico
Rumania
Russia
Scotland
South Africa
Spain
Surinam
Sweden
Switzerland
Tahiti and the
  French Islands of
  the Pacific
Taiwan
Thailand
Turkey
Venezuela
Wales
West Germany
Yugoslavia

PICTURE CREDITS

The publishers wish to thank the following for the use of the photographs used in this book: *Guinness Book of World Records* for some of the animal pictures; *Holland Herald* magazine, Amsterdam; International Telephone & Telegraph Company, New York; Robert and Martha Murray Sumwalt, New York; and the Surinam Tourist Bureau. Special thanks are extended to Mr. John H. Nelson, Director, Surinam Tourist Bureau, New York, for his invaluable aid in the preparation of this book.

Copyright © 1971 by Sterling Publishing Co., Inc.
419 Park Avenue South, New York, N.Y. 10016
British edition published by Oak Tree Press Co., Ltd., Nassau, Bahamas
Distributed in Australia by Oak Tree Press Co., Ltd.,
P.O. Box 34, Brickfield Hill, Sydney 2000, N.S.W.
Distributed in the United Kingdom and elsewhere in the British Commonwealth
by Ward Lock Ltd., 116 Baker Street, London W 1

Manufactured in the United States of America
All rights reserved
Library of Congress Catalog Card No.: 70-167670
ISBN 0–8069–1146–8   UK 7061 2338–7
1147–6

In a Bush Negro village, a woman carries firewood home on her head.

CONTENTS

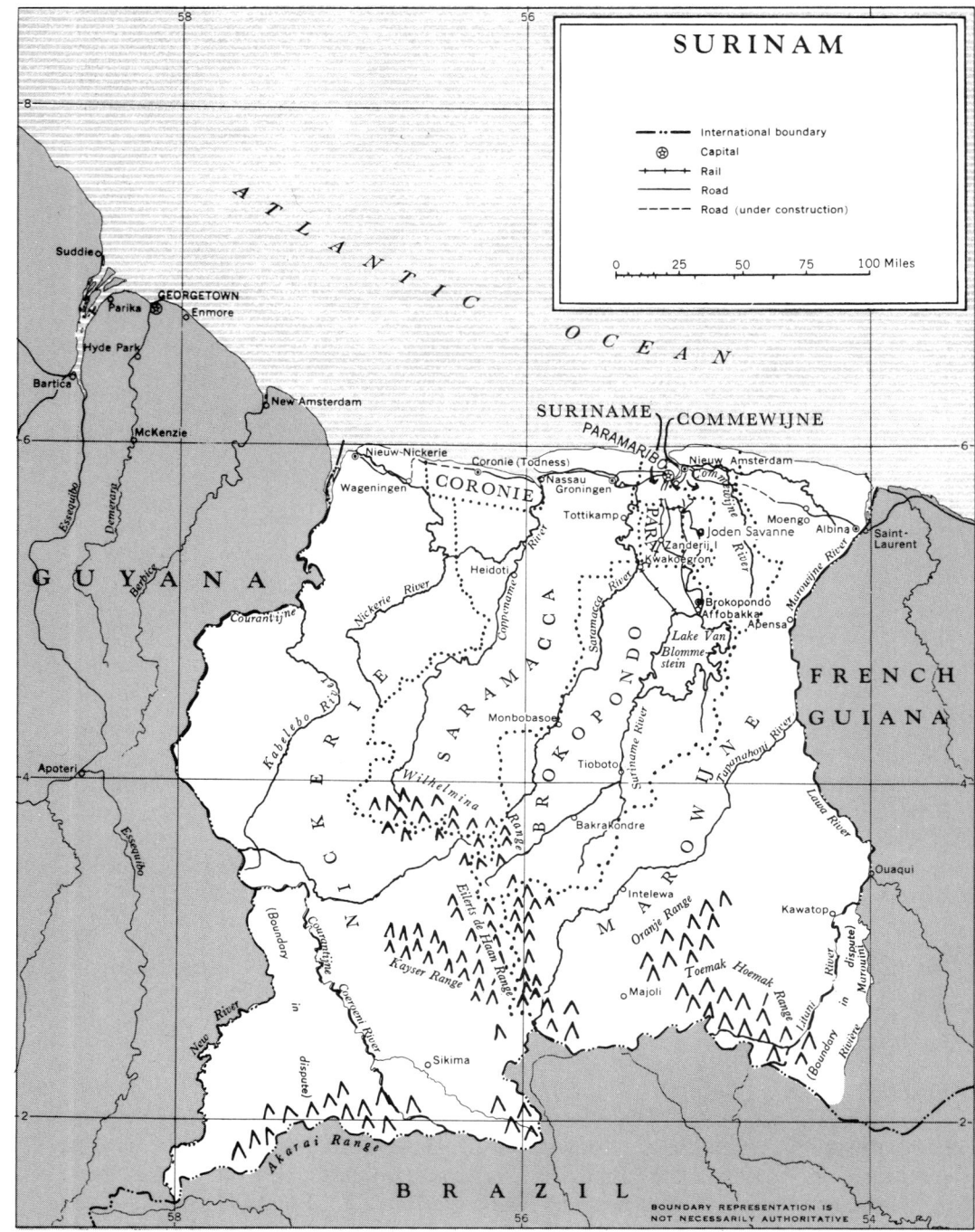

SURINAM

International boundary
Capital
Rail
Road
Road (under construction)

0   25   50   75   100 Miles

ATLANTIC

OCEAN

Suddie

GEORGETOWN

Parika

Enmore

Hyde Park

Bartica

New Amsterdam

McKenzie

GUYANA

SURINAME   COMMEWIJNE

PARAMARIBO

Nieuw Amsterdam

Nieuw-Nickerie   Coronie (Todness)

Wageningen   CORONIE   Nassau
Groningen

Tottikamp   PIR   Moengo
Joden Savanne   Albina   Saint-
Laurent
Heidoti   Zanderij, I
Swakoegron

Brokopondo
Affobakka   Apensa

Lake Van
Blomme-
stein

Monbobasoe

FRENCH

GUIANA

Tioboto

Bakrakondre

Intelewa

Ouaqui

Kawatop

Majoli

Sikima

Akarai Range

BRAZIL

BOUNDARY REPRESENTATION IS
NOT NECESSARILY AUTHORITATIVE   54

Essequibo
Demerara
Berbice
Courantijne
Nickerie River
Kabelebo River
Coppename River
Saramacca River
Suriname River
Marowijne River
Tapanahoni River
Lawa River
New River
Courantijne
Gwen-ani River
Itany River
Marouini
Wilhelmina Range
Eilerts de Haan Range
Kayser Range
Oranje Range
Toemak Hoemak Range
NICKERIE
SARAMACCA
BROKOPONDO
MAROWIJNE
Apoteri
(Boundary in dispute)
(Boundary in dispute)

Surinam's chief man-made waterway is the Saramacca Canal connecting Paramaribo with Nassau, on the coast 50 miles to the west.

I. LAND

THE TERRITORY of Surinam, also called Dutch Guiana, is a free integral part of the Kingdom of the Netherlands, located on the northeast coast of South America, between the Orinoco and Amazon River valleys. Bounded on the west by Guyana (formerly British Guiana), on the east by French Guiana, and on the south by Brazil, Surinam has a coastline on the north approximately 215 miles long. The total area, including a region claimed by Guyana, is about 62,000 square miles, just about the size of Oklahoma or twice the size of Portugal.

The border dispute with Guyana dates back to a treaty made in the early 19th century, in which the left bank of the Courantijne (the "ij" in Dutch is pronounced "y") River was desig-nated as Surinam's western boundary. A difference of opinion lies in the exact location of the river source. Guyana claims it is the Coeroeni River, while Surinam says it is the New River, which lies considerably to the west of the Coeroeni.

NATURAL REGIONS

Three major geographic regions extend latitudinally across the territory of Surinam: coastal lowlands, grassy savannahs, or plains, and mountain rain forests.

COASTAL LOWLANDS

Numerous rivers fan out from the interior, bringing down great quantities of fertile soil,

With so many waterways, ferries are a common means of transport. Here passengers board the Maratacca ferry.

making the coastal plain one of the most important agricultural regions in the territory. More than 80 per cent of the people still live along the coast, where the early colonists first built their plantations.

This flat, swampy land, much of which is under water at high tide, contains shellfish and valuable mineral deposits. The farmland is protected by an extensive system of dykes and canals.

SAVANNAHS

South of the coastal lowlands is a 10- to 50-mile-wide band of loamy soil. Most of this area is covered with grass, low shrubs, and scattered trees, but the white sand lies exposed in many places. Small farmers have built their villages near the banks of the wide rivers, which roll down from the highlands to the sea.

MOUNTAIN RAIN FORESTS

About 75 per cent of the country is hilly and

Police Headquarters in Paramaribo is located on the bank of the Suriname River.

heavily forested. South of the savannah are rolling sandstone hills, which gradually rise to small mountains on the Brazilian border. The highest peak is Juliana Top (4,200 feet) in the Wilhelmina Range.

RIVERS

Two of the rivers form Surinam's borders— the Courantijne to the west and the Marowijne to the east, which is shared with French Guiana. Originating in the rain forests, Surinam's swift, brown rivers, interrupted by eddies, rapids, and waterfalls, tumble northward to the ocean. A few miles south of the shoreline, they turn westward, blocked by silt deposits, which ocean currents coming from the mouth of the Amazon have deposited. Mud flats run out from the coast about a mile, making it hard to tell just where the land begins or ends.

Surinam's four major rivers are the Saramacca, Nickerie, Suriname and Coppename. The Coppename reaches the Atlantic Ocean at Nassau, while the Nickerie and Saramacca stream north from the Wilhelmina Range. Among the tributaries of the Courantijne are the Coeroeni and the Kabelebo.

On Surinam's eastern border, a number of rivers, including the Tapanahoni, connect with the Marowijne, which empties into a delta near Albina. The new Affobakka Dam holds back the waters of the mighty Suriname and Saramacca Rivers to form Lake Van Blommestein.

CLIMATE

Temperatures are stable, with the average ranging from about 78 to 83 degrees F. the year round. Northeast trade winds keep the coastal region from being too hot or humid. Still, most people rest for a while during the warmest part of the day.

September is the hottest month, and January the coolest. There are two rainy seasons each

The damming of the Suriname River at Affobakka created a large lake, part of which we see here.

year, from April to July and from November to February. Rain falls most frequently on hillsides facing the ocean.

FLORA AND FAUNA

South America contains many varieties of living things, some not found in North America. Moreover, the "Three Guianas," lying between the Amazon and the Atlantic, are extremely isolated. Understandably then, this isolation from other South American countries accounts for even more unusual plant and animal species.

PLANTS

The swamps, savannahs, and jungles of Surinam contain over 3,500 different kinds of plant life, including palms, giant ferns, hardwood and tropical-fruit trees. Thick, ropelike lianas (vines) rooted in the ground, climb up round many tree trunks and are powerful enough to strangle a tree. Air plants (mosses, lichens, orchids) also grow on other plants, but get their food from the atmosphere.

Along the coastline, clawlike mangrove roots reach down into muddy waters, while razor-

Another agricultural product of Surinam is the orange—not a native tree, but introduced from the Old World.

sharp saw grass fringes the marshland ponds. If left alone, these mangrove trees will send forth aerial prop roots that will eventually form tangled swamps and then project small aprons of land into the Atlantic. In the inland waterways float huge water lilies, with pads big enough to support a small child. And farther inland, vivid masses of red, orange, and purple bougainvillea tumble over the dense foliage, which includes flowering shrubs such as frangipani (often mistaken for jasmine because of its resemblance to this voluptuous flower). Masses of yellow flowers crown the bare branches of the acacia tree, making a brilliant contrast against the electric-blue sky.

Branches of dark green "hipponai" grow in tiers like evergreens. At the end of each tier hangs a fringe of crimson blossoms. Among the various creepers that garland the trees are the

The lush vegetation of Surinam includes many exotic plants, such as the Rode Paloeloe *(the national flower of Surinam), shown here.*

purple peaflower and a flaming red-spiked variety.

Some plants fill the air with a perfume almost too powerful. The sweet scent of the flowers of honeysuckle, the flamboyant tree, and the large yellow vanilla vine can be detected miles away. Other sources of fragrance are the resins. The white resin from the "hayawa" tree is almost like incense, while that of the "tauranera" imitates and surpasses that of the vanilla vine.

Among the many varieties of palm trees is the wild plantain, a cousin of the Madagascar traveller's palm, which stores rain water throughout the dry season. Bamboo grows mostly in the inhabited areas of the territory.

Beneath the trees grow delicate begonias, multicolored caladiums, fragile calla lilies, and red passion flowers. Heartier jungle plants are the scarlet ixora (named after a Hindu divinity), hibiscus, yellow, funnel-shaped allamanda, and red bottle brush, all familiar to Florida residents.

Some tree trunks are enormous, many of them having numerous buttresses radiating from a common root. The largest of these trees is the mora (found only in Trinidad and the three Guianas).

MAMMALS

Vegetation is so profuse in many parts of the jungle that it has crowded out many animals. Still, in a tropical country with a sparse human population and varied physical features, animal life is almost sure to be abundant. The government encourages foreigners to come to Surinam on jungle tours to photograph and/or hunt the many wild animals.

Rodents like the paca, agouti, and capybara are the most predominant mammals. The paca is a large guinea pig with brown and white spotted skin, found mostly along river banks. There it nestles in hollow logs, going out to forage at night. The agouti, more like a rabbit with black whiskers, coarse brown hair, and powerful hind legs, dwells in the forest, venturing to the water only when it has to drink. It feeds during the day on fallen fruit. Also living along river banks is the world's largest rodent, the shy capybara. Perhaps because of its un-

Even a grown man would have no trouble standing on one of these giant water-lily pads. Although they flourish in most rivers and lagoons of the Amazon Basin, Surinam is especially endowed with them.

9

The artfully camouflaged jaguar (above) resembles a leopard in appearance, but lacks that animal's grace. The tapir (below) often the prey of the jaguar, is a strict vegetarian like his distant relatives, the horse and rhinoceros. The jaguar is the largest of the New World cats and the tapir is the largest of all South American land mammals. While the tapir is shy, the jaguar represents a threat to be pacified.

The capybara, a playful, webbed-toed animal, is closely related to the guinea pig. This animal has the distinction of being the world's largest living rodent. The capybara, like the tapir, is extremely shy.

willingness to mix with other jungle mammals, it is an excellent swimmer.

Another striking mammal is the tapir, a relative of the rhinoceros, with a thick neck, heavy body, slender legs, and long flexible snout. This large, cautious animal has a keen sense of smell and hearing and feeds in the dark. For all its staunch appearance though, the tapir, like the capybara, would rather run away than fight.

Other mammals include the bat, sloth, anteater and bony-plated armadillo. The busy anteater uses his long, thin nose and quick tongue to raid ant hills and rotten wood, while the lazy sloth spends its life hanging back downward from a tree. The clever armadillo merely rolls up into a hard shell when afraid.

Most prominent of the bats is the huge fruit-eater, with a wing-span up to 3 feet. The blood-sucking vampire is a smaller bat, whose attacks on other animals are so serious that it is impossible to keep chickens in Surinam except by shutting them up at night.

In addition to familiar animals like the fox, skunk, deer, squirrel, raccoon, otter, weasel, puma, ocelot, and opossum, there is the margay, a small, black-spotted cat with a tail almost as long as its body.

Most cats are called "tigers" in Surinam. While these tiger-cats are common, they are rarely seen, since they are afraid of other animals. It is strange, but the natives have chosen diverse animals—the tapir, jaguar, and capybara—to worship as sacred creatures. Many Amerindians are extremely fearful of jaguars, however. In many Amerindian homes you will see strings of jaguar teeth and skins hung there to keep the live ones away.

The peccary, or bush hog, is far more fierce. One variety called "pingo" roams the woods in packs up to 200, eating everything in sight. If a hunter takes refuge in a tree, these wild boars wait patiently until he starves or is rescued. It is dangerous to harm these animals for they can do serious damage with their tusks.

Other night prowlers are the coati (which sleeps with its nose pressed against its stomach) and the long-tailed kinkajou (honey bear). Both are members of the raccoon family. There are also several kinds of ant bears, the largest of which is a strange-looking animal about the size of a bloodhound. But this fierce-looking animal has a big bushy tail under which it takes shelter. If pressed the ant bear will defend itself against man by hugging him close and pressing long claws into the human body. The tree porcupine, with its bulging black eyes and large pink nose, likes to play in trees. It is well fitted for this clowning, having a long tail that it uses as a fifth hand.

The jungle has many eerie sounds such as the constant drip of water, drone of locusts,

In contrast to their huge elephant moths and blood-sucking vampire bats, Surinam's jungles also contain the hummingbird who, even when gorging himself, weighs no more than 1/18th of an ounce.

croaking of frogs, and crashing of tree branches. One of the most startling noises, however, is the frenzied cry of the red howling monkey. Chattering monkeys and baboons range in size from the 4-foot-high "quarta," with its smooth face and long black hair to the tiny golden "sinkanee." Bright-hued "sackawinkis" swing single-file through the trees in herds.

BIRDS

Other noisy creatures in Surinam include the brightly colored parrots, macaws, and toucans. The toucan has an extraordinarily large, down-turned beak resembling a lobster claw and yelps like a hurt puppy. The snow-crested bellbird sounds like the iron clapper of a bell. The calfbird makes cowlike sounds, while the goatsucker moans throughout the night in mournful tones. Hawks shriek and mocking birds scream, while parakeets and other birds chatter. The ever-present kiskadee and "pi-piyo" cry out their own names incessantly.

Since the coastline of Surinam is swampy, there are not many sea birds, but there are many other water birds—terns, rails, snipes, herons, egrets, ducks, and razorbills (a species of auk). The long-necked snakebird dives under the water for his food.

The scarlet ibis, pink flamingo, orange pheasant, hummingbird, cock-of-the-rock, and brilliant bird of paradise add still more coloration to the jungle. The vivid orange and red cock-of-the-rock dances on a rock with its wings spread and its tail jerking up and down.

Game birds include quail, pigeon, and the partridgelike "maam."

Over 600 varieties of birds have been counted in Surinam, from the huge black vulture to the tiniest bright hummingbird.

INSECTS

People find it best not to lie on the grass or lean against trees in Surinam, since all manner of insects abound, including sandflies, scorpions, and spiders (some as big as matchboxes). There are also pen-sized grasshoppers. Giant fireflies glow in the dark, while dragonflies soar backwards and forwards like miniature helicopters.

Butterflies as big as saucers flit through forest skies. The most spectacular of these insects is a brilliant, sapphire-blue beauty called the "morphus adonis." With all this available, butterfly netting is a popular pastime in Surinam, especially among the Arawak Indians.

A profusion of insects also live in the earth. Aztec ants build large underground nests and canals, while termites construct their black, bulb-shaped homes in trees or hills. Meat-

The anteater is one of Surinam's many unusual native mammals.

eating ants attack weak animals, while driver ants come in 5-foot-wide armies to steal supplies. Finally, there are the umbrella ants, who can strip a tree of foliage overnight. They do this by arriving in swarms, snipping small pieces of leaves from the unfortunate tree, and flipping the maimed leaf segments over their heads into grooves on their foreheads.

FISH

The Amazon-Orinoco River basin is one of the world's most plentiful sources for freshwater tropical fish, from the tiny guppy and pencilfish to the huge arapaima, which grows to 15 feet in length and 500 pounds in weight. In addition to giant catfish, sting rays, and electric eels, there are barbudos (bearded fish), prize peacock bass, air-breathing lungfish, and fish that leap like salmon. Surinam also has the world's most savage fish, the sharp-toothed piranhas, who by the hundreds can reduce a man to a skeleton in minutes. Ocean fish include tarpon as big as 6 feet long and 100 pounds.

Among Surinam's strange water creatures are the white river porpoise that lives below the rapids and a fish that is born with a film over its eyes. Also in its waterways is the lumbering, barrel-shaped manatee (seacow), which rolls its eyes like a flirting mermaid. A monstrous turtle lies camouflaged on the river bottom waiting for victims, which it sucks up like a vacuum cleaner through its long, snakelike throat.

Foot travellers in Surinam's tropical rain forests must be wary of this spider. When fully extended, this killer is capable of spanning the length of a husky man's forearm. Furthermore, birds, swallowed whole, are a staple of this spider's diet.

REPTILES

Dangerous Surinamese reptiles, many of which are considered sacred, include the rattlesnake, anaconda, emerald tree boa, and boa constrictor. The long-fanged bushmaster, which attacks without provocation, often lives in the same hole with the armadillo, while the gentle, nonpoisonous cribo is popular with snake-charmers.

Water snakes attack the lazy cayman alligator while it sleeps in the mud. Caymans have a habit of slapping their tails on the water to attract fish. When the tail of a lizard is torn off, it grows a new one from the injured spot. Probably the best-known lizard is the tree-dwelling, plant-eating iguana, which has a jagged, raised ridge along its back like a dinosaur. Many Surinamese are fond of iguana eggs and meat.

This miniature replica of the earth's prehistoric animals, the iguana, is zestfully hunted by the Amerindians. Its succulent, roasted meat has the taste and consistency of tender young chicken. The iguana himself likes nothing better than to feast on turtle eggs.

Other lizards are the zebra-striped skink, the night-roaming gecko (so called from its cry), and the "tegu," which for some reason lays its eggs in termite nests. There are giant toads, which croak endlessly. The flat-headed Surinam toad has a unique manner of raising its young. The baby toads live on the back of the female until they are large enough to care for themselves. The rough skin of this animal often contains glands poisonous to humans.

Operation Gamba, which rescued over 10,000 animals otherwise doomed to drown by flooding while the Affobakka Dam was being built was the most dangerous project of its kind ever attempted. But it provided scientists with much important data about the animals living in Surinam's rain forest.

CITIES AND DISTRICTS

Surinam is divided into eight districts, each governed by a commissioner: Suriname, Para, Marowijne, Commewijne, Brokopondo, Nickerie, Coronie and Saramacca.

Besides these, there is the important city district of Paramaribo with a federal status like that of Washington, D.C.

SURINAME AND PARA DISTRICTS

The Suriname district surrounds the capital city and includes the land just below the mouth of the Suriname River. Here, most of the industry of the territory is concentrated.

Just south and to the west of this district is Para, known for its huge bauxite mines and for busy Zanderij Airport. The main road south of the capital splices both districts as it passes by the big Bruynzeel plywood factory and services several large bauxite-refining plants.

Zanderij Airfield, 30 miles south of Paramaribo boasts one of the longest and smoothest runways in South America. Moreover, it is served regularly by international airlines.

Further inland, across the gold fields, is the remarkable Princess Juliana Mission Hospital. Built in the jungle with the aid of voluntary contributions, it is operated by the Evangelical Community of Brethren.

PARAMARIBO DISTRICT

The capital, Paramaribo, is both a city and an autonomous zone surrounded by Suriname district. Located on the banks of the Suriname River about 12 miles from the ocean, it is also a thriving port.

Here most of the buildings, including even the Roman Catholic cathedral, are made of wood. In the Old Section, small Dutch-colonial-style wooden houses with dormer windows, sharp-pitched roofs, peaked gables, and inviting verandas decked with flowers line the shady streets. Most traffic problems are caused by scooters, bicycles, two-wheeled donkey carts, and *bromfiets* or motorcycles.

Official government life focusses around the Oranjeplein, on which are located the white, clapboard Governor's Mansion and the red-brick, colonial finance building, built in the 18th century with bricks brought over as ballast for sailing vessels. Just off the square is the Staten Building, where Parliament meets, and a 200-year-old structure housing offices of the minister-president.

A ship docks at Paramaribo on the Suriname River. The city is located about 12 miles south of the Atlantic Ocean.

Paramaribo's wooden houses have often been burnt to the ground. Watermolenstraat, seen here, has many typical Surinam-style houses. You can see, too, that cars drive to the left in Surinam, a diehard reflection of the days when Britain owned the territory (before 1667) and all carts and foot traffic flowed on the left sides of lanes and thoroughfares.

Clouds drift above Paramaribo as ships lie quietly in dock on the Suriname River.

Everyone shops for fresh vegetables and fruits in Paramaribo's open-air market.

Several blocks south is the main business section and various houses of worship. The busy market is an excellent spot to study the habits and costume of these picturesque people. Women carry produce (fish, chickens, fruit, peanuts, vegetables) in trays balanced on their heads. After they have sold these items, they are likely to walk home balancing their purchases on their heads.

On the north side of town, along the river front, are Fort Zeelandia and several old homes nestled under huge tamarind trees. Once used as a prison, the fort has been converted into a museum.

Fearful that modern architecture would cause the capital to lose its unique character, a group of interested citizens have organized their efforts to see that important buildings retain their original style. When the old Court of Justice building (1793) was restored in 1824, the new roof did not conform to the old design. The building has been remodelled again, using the original blueprint from the Dutch archives.

The government recently issued a series of stamps commemorating its antiquities, which included the old Jewish settlement of Joden Savanne. It plans to rebuild the synagogue and repolish the engravings on the tombstones.

MAROWIJNE DISTRICT

The easternmost district, Marowijne, which borders on French Guiana, can be reached from the capital by car, boat, or plane. A good road, which passes by several primitive settlements, connects Moengo, built in 1928 by the Surinam

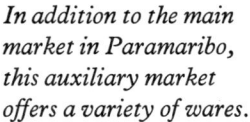

In addition to the main market in Paramaribo, this auxiliary market offers a variety of wares.

16

The C.K.C. Department Store, largest in Paramaribo, is housed in a 200-year-old colonial building.

Bauxite Company, with Albina on the French border.

While Albina is the administrative seat, Moengo is the most important town since Alcoa's bauxite mines and huge processing plants are located here. Freighters carry the bauxite down Surinam's winding rivers to the sea. Moengo is a prosperous town with schools, stores, churches, a hospital, wide streets, and attractive homes.

Other natives of Marowijne make their living by fishing, lumbering, gold-mining, or extracting balata gum, a rubber product made from the sap of the wild bully tree.

Directly across the river from Albina is the small but infamous town of St. Laurent, site of

Albina, on the Marowijne River was once a trading post for gold miners and collectors of balata gum, used for insulating telephone cables and making golf balls. (See also p. 58 for picture of Surinamese men collecting this sticky treasure.) Across the river, in French Guiana, is the former penal colony of St. Laurent du Maroni (Maroni being the French spelling for the river).

At Nieuw Amsterdam, a 17th-century fort at the mouth of the Suriname River has been turned into an open-air museum, which includes the reconstructed Bush Negro village seen here.

the former French penal colony. Albina is also the take-off point for jungle safaris up the river into the interior.

COMMEWIJNE DISTRICT

Easily reached from Paramaribo by auto-ferry and a short car ride, this district is occupied mostly by Javanese sugar and fruit growers, who have retained many of their native traditions. In the administrative town of Nieuw Amsterdam, located at the junction of the Suriname and Commewijne Rivers, is an old fort, whose grounds have been made into an open-air museum, illustrating the history, natural life, and various life styles of Surinam. Along the river front are pillboxes used to protect the country against German attacks during World War II.

BROKOPONDO DISTRICT

The major key to Surinam's future lies in Brokopondo, which demonstrates the efficiency and drive of these enterprising people. Completion of a gigantic flood control dam across the Suriname River at Affobakka in 1965 began turning generators to provide more electric power for home and industry. This feat made it possible for a much larger portion of the aluminium-producing process to take place in Surinam.

NICKERIE DISTRICT

Separated from Guyana by the Courantijne River is Nickerie, also a major rice-growing district, where the government has reclaimed thousands of acres through extensive drainage systems.

After land was reclaimed from the sea and cleared (as had been done in Holland) for the giant Wageningen Project in 1949, a new town sprang up almost overnight. On this vast acreage of reclaimed polderland, farmers use all mechanized methods for planting, harvesting, and transportation of rice. Large bauxite deposits recently discovered in the interior promise rapid development of the district.

CORONIE DISTRICT

East of Nickerie, on the Atlantic coast, is Coronie, the palm garden of Surinam. In this district, a predominantly Creole population harvests coconuts and processes them for oil, used in cooking. The copra (coconut) meat is used mainly as fodder for pigs. Watching barefoot pickers shimmy up tall, swaying palm trees and send coconuts crashing to the ground is a popular pastime for tourists.

Coronie can be reached by several routes. The most picturesque trip, however, is the one from Nickerie that passes through gorgeous jungle growth and quaint Indian villages.

SARAMACCA DISTRICT

Oil was recently discovered near the coast in this district, which embraces coastal lowlands, savannahs, and the highest mountain peak in the country. Once the home of flourishing plantations, Saramacca's lowlands are now dominated by small Indonesian and Hindustani farmers. Rice is their major crop, followed by citrus fruits, soy beans, and coconuts. In the district headquarters town of Groningen, near the mouth of the Saramacca River, a monument marks a doomed colonization expedition undertaken by Dutch farmers in 1845.

JUNGLE SAFARIS

Surinam has just finished building a series of airstrips and guest houses along the shores of its remote jungle rivers so that visitors will be able to see the variety of life in its interior.

The first lodge built, at Stoelman's Island on the French Guiana border, can be reached either from Paramaribo or Albina by plane or car and boat. In Albina, you can hire a canoe-like *proa*, or a small motorboat with a canopy of palm leaves and an outboard motor. A competent crew will point out Amerindian and Bush Negro villages along the river banks.

At Stoelman's Island, you can rent a handsomely carved dugout canoe with Bush Negro oarsmen. It is an exciting experience to watch these highly skilled boatsmen manoeuvre their long slender boats through rapids and around waterfalls.

A baby capybara relaxes at Nieuw Amsterdam's open-air museum.

In Vailliant Plein, a large square in Paramaribo, this monument commemorates the founding of Surinam.

2. HISTORY

PRE-COLUMBIAN ERA

The Guianas claim to have been the realm of El Dorado. This legendary Indian prince at least once a year covered himself with gold dust and dove into the sacred lake of Manoa. Both Spanish conquistadores and English explorers searched for gold hidden in the jungles of Guiana (including the famous Sir Walter Raleigh who actually did pinpoint Manoa—minus its gold-bedded lake).

Nothing is certain about the origin of American Indians, but most anthropologists believe that they are a Mongoloid people who came to the Western Hemisphere by way of the Bering Strait and Alaska. Supposedly, they reached the southern tip of South America about 5,000 years ago. A more recent theory insists that some of them migrated from Asia, sailing eastward across the Pacific and pausing long enough in their journeys to settle the Polynesian Islands. But even those who hold this sea theory agree that a large-scale migration by this route seems unlikely.

Since the Guianas are warm and wet, with a rapid decay rate, few artifacts from earlier civilizations remain. It is believed, however, that the culture of these Indians never reached the high peaks of the Inca, Aztec, or Mayan peoples. While evidence has been found of weaving and pottery making, there are no remnants of permanent architecture. Obviously, they lived in caves or thatched huts.

Burial urns and middens (shell mounds) containing human bones have been found in the coastal lowlands near Nieuw Amsterdam (Commewijne district). Archeologists have also identified a stone axe, whose head was carved in the shape of a capybara.

The general conclusions are that these burial mounds were not made by permanent residents, but by strangers who came from the sea—in all probability, the Carib Indians. Examination of the different layers of soil showed that the sites were not occupied continuously, but instead on infrequent though repeated occasions.

When the first Europeans arrived, the resident Guianese tribes—the Arawaks, Waurás, and Wapisianas—were all united by a common aversion to the Caribs, whom Indian legends say came from the sea. It is impossible to determine when, or from where, the early native tribes came to Guiana. However, they seem to have been there when the bloodthirsty Caribs arrived.

According to one theory, the Caribs went by land from the jungles of Brazil to the Antilles (Caribbean) Islands, where they were found by the first European explorers. They seem to have reached the Guianas at the end of the 15th century—about the same time that Columbus and the other first Europeans came.

Mysterious rock carvings have been found on Temehri Rick in the Courantijne River. One shallow engraving shows a 13-foot-high rectangular figure with a crown. Two rock drawings were also found on a boulder in a tributary of the Courantijne. Perhaps significantly, most of these rocks are located near rapids or waterfalls. Some have crude drawings of men, snakes, monkeys, and other animals.

Today's Indians seem to know little about these rock etchings. They say either that women made them or that they are the work of God's Son, who drew them with His finger while

Two handsome colonial buildings in Paramaribo are, at the left, the Ministry of General Affairs or Office of the Prime Minister, built in 1773, and at right, the Staten Building (17th century), where the Parliament of Surinam has sat for over 100 years.

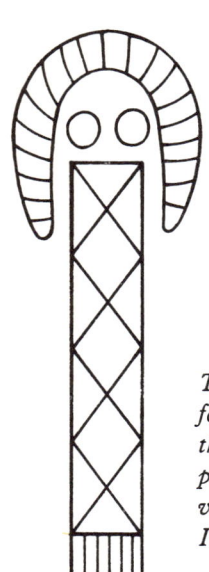

This ancient rock engraving, found on a granite slab in the Courantijne River, probably had a magical value to the early Arawak Indians who carved it.

wandering on earth. When the German naturalist-explorer Humboldt asked about them in the 18th century, he was told that the occult drawings were done long ago by Indian forefathers. Subsequent explorers received the same vague answer.

When the first Europeans came, they found the peaceful Arawak farmers, who lived in permanent communities along Guiana's northern river banks, being weakened by the fierce Caribs who periodically raided their villages and carried away their women as slaves.

The Indian word Arawak means "meal-eater," while Carib means "brave stranger." From the latter is derived the word *Cribal* or "cannibal," used by Columbus to describe these warlike people. Excellent canoe-makers, the Caribs were one of the first Indian groups in the Americas to use sails on their vessels.

Arawak villages were composed of several related families, who lived in large thatched-roof dwellings. Each little settlement was protected by a moat or palisade. In addition to the animals that they hunted, with blow-guns and

Most of Surinam's American Indians, or Amerindians as they are called, live in the interior. These people in traditional costume are Caribs, one of the main aboriginal groups.

poisoned arrows, the Arawak diet consisted of cassava (tapioca), arrowroot (a starchy root plant), sugar cane, squash, maize (corn), beans and yams. They also grew cotton and wove material on looms. Little clothing was necessary, but they made bark-cloth garments to wear on ceremonial occasions.

Despite more than 400 years of contact with European civilization most of the descendants of these Indians have changed their way of life very little. In fact, the majority choose to live in remote areas of the interior.

DISCOVERY AND COLONIZATION

While Columbus was probably the first European to sight the Guiana coast (in 1498), there is no record of his having gone ashore. Spanish explorer Alonso de Ojeda is commemorated as the discoverer of the Guianas, but little was known about the region until Domingo de Vera claimed it for Spain in 1593.

During the following century, both Spanish and Portuguese adventurers tried to establish colonies, but soon lost interest when they discovered no large caches of gold. In 1630, Englishmen built a fort at Toriaca on the banks of the Suriname River (near the present capital), but the small settlement did not last.

Several years later, the French attempted to colonize Surinam but found that the terrain, climate, and Indians were more than they could manage. But in 1650 the governor of Barbados was Lord Willoughby of Parham, a wealthy English Royalist who had been exiled by Oliver Cromwell. It was Willoughby who finally succeeded in establishing a permanent colony in Surinam. Receiving a friendly welcome from the Indians, this determined man made treaties with them, rebuilt a fort the French had built, set up plantations, and welcomed settlers from the island of Cayenne (now part of French Guiana). Jewish refugees from Europe and Portuguese-controlled Brazil also brought their capital and skills to the plantation economy. Later, in 1665, the Dutch gave them a tract of land on which to build a synagogue.

Willoughby's prosperous colony was based on the work of slaves imported from Africa. The British settlers in Surinam traded mostly with England and the West Indian Islands.

Soon after the colony was granted to Willoughby, trouble began in Europe in the form of wars among the Dutch, French, and English. The conflict soon spread to the New World, although Peter Stuyvesant, the Governor-General of the Dutch colony of New Amsterdam (today New York), was unaware of it. In 1664, he welcomed a British battleship with open arms, only to be forced to give up his colony within minutes. When a peace treaty was signed at Breda, Holland, in 1667, the British were so remorseful at having tricked the Dutch that they gave Surinam to the Netherlands as a salve to their consciences for keeping New York. Both English and French settlers were allowed to

23

remain in Surinam and keep their property in return for allegiance and contributions to the Dutch crown. It did not work out

After a short while, the British fleet once more captured the Dutch fort at Surinam, levelled plantations, and took Englishmen back to Jamaica. The Dutch managed, however, to regain control of the fort within the year. During this era of confused authority, the Indians grew even more hostile. Guiana became such a burden to the Dutch crown that it was sold to a group supported by the City of Amsterdam, the Dutch West Indian Company. A nobleman, Cornelius Van Aessens, the lord of Sommelsdijk, took over as Governor.

The new governor did much to bring stability to the colony. Laws were passed forbidding cruelty to slaves; the government was to conduct trials and mete out punishment. While most people liked Governor Van Aessens, his soldiers did not because he demanded too much from them. A military group revolted, killed the governor, and took over control of the colony. Plantation owners struck back by executing the army rebels.

The colony continued to change hands between the English and Dutch until 1815, when the government of Holland resolutely took over, finally putting an end to 200 years of shifting authority.

Meanwhile, the French were demanding tribute from the Surinamese colonists. To avoid paying it, many plantation owners hid

In Paramaribo, this bust commemorates Lieutenant Eilerts de Haan, who led an expedition up the Courantijne River in 1910. This Dutch naval officer is so esteemed that the Surinamese named a mountain chain in the south-central section after him.

their slaves in the forest. These black men joined with slaves who had previously escaped. Their descendants, the Marrons or Bush Negroes, remained at war with the European settlers for many years afterward.

When slavery was finally abolished in 1863, plantation owners suffered greatly from the loss of a cheap, permanent supply of workers. As a result, they began to import workers from Asia under a contract (indenture) whereby the workers' fare was to be paid back by deduction

This monument in Paramaribo commemorates the men of Surinam who served with the Allies in World War II.

A landmark in the heart of Paramaribo is a statue of India's great leader, Mahatma Gandhi. One of the giants of the 20th century, Gandhi is held in high esteem by all the people of Surinam, whether of Indian origin or not. The statue is set on a pedestal in the middle of a pool.

from their wages. The first immigrants to arrive were Chinese from Hong Kong. Next came thousands of East Indians (Hindustanis), followed by Javanese workers from Indonesia. This wide assortment of people from five different continents has made Surinam one of the unique places of the world.

Surinam remained a Dutch crown colony until self-rule was granted in 1866. It received more home freedom in 1937 when its status was changed to a *territory* of the Netherlands. And during World War II, while the Netherlands was occupied by the Nazis, Surinam remained loyal to the Allies and invited the United States to establish bases there.

After the war, in 1950, the territory was granted a new constitution, making it a fairly self-sufficient commonwealth.

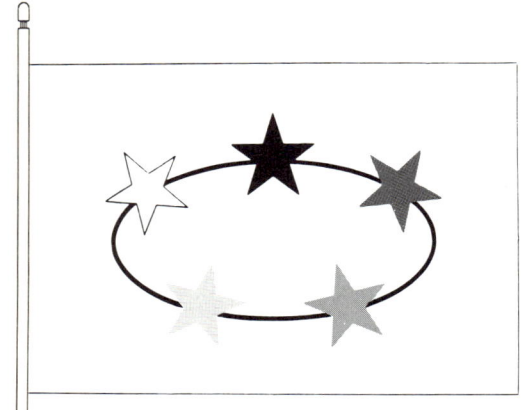

The flag of Surinam shows a ring of five stars on a white field, representing the territory's most important ethnic constituents. There is a white star for the Europeans, a black one for the Africans, a brown one for the Hindustanis and Javanese, a yellow one for the Chinese, and a red one for the Amerindians.

The official seal of Surinam says in Latin, "Justice, Piety, Faith."

JUSTITIA   PIETAS   FIDES

The handsome Governor's Palace dominates the Oranjeplein in the heart of old Paramaribo.

3. GOVERNMENT

IN 1942, QUEEN WILHELMINA of the Netherlands had promised the people of Surinam a new political status at the end of World War II. The 1954 Charter guaranteed the territory of Surinam equal footing in the Kingdom along with Holland and the Netherlands Antilles islands of Aruba, Bonaire, Curaçao, Saba, St. Eustatius, and St. Maärten.

All internal affairs are settled by the Surinamese themselves, while matters of defence, which affect the entire Kingdom, are decided by all the partners together. Common interests of the territories are managed by the Council of the Realm at The Hague, at which all are represented.

Surinam is an associate member of the European Common Market (EEC) by virtue of its ties with the Netherlands, which is a full member.

Surinam is a parliamentary democracy, with a Governor appointed by the Queen to represent her interests. Nine cabinet members, each elected for four years, make up the executive branch, which is led by a Prime-Minister–President.

The people elect 36 representatives to sit in the Staten, a single-house parliament. Three representatives are elected by direct vote from each of the 8 local districts, and 12 by the territory at large on a proportional basis.

Local government is virtually nonexistent, since all authority rests with the executive and legislative branches in the capital. District commissioners are appointed by the government.

The Ministry of Finance, housed in the old town hall, is a fine example of colonial architecture.

JUDICIARY

The judiciary is made up of local courts and the Supreme Court, with judges appointed by the Governor and serving for life. Holland passes few laws that apply to her territories. In fact, separation of authority has become so complete since 1950 that Holland now knows little about the internal affairs of her overseas territories. Surinam is responsible for its own public works, education, public health, and social legislation.

POLITICS

Soon after World War II, local leaders brought the races together into an organization called *Unie Suriname*. At the time of the first general election in 1949, four parties represented the three major ethnic groups in Surinam—Creoles, Hindustanis, and Indonesians.

The Governor of Surinam, Johan Henri Ferrier (left), receives a visitor in the 18th-century Governor's Mansion.

Facing the Oranjeplein, Paramaribo's historic old square, are the Ministry of Home Affairs (foreground) and the Ministry of Finance (with tower). The latter building is the city's former town hall.

There are now several political parties, among which are the National Party of Surinam (NPS), the PNP (which broke off from the NPS), the United Hindustani Party (UHP), and the SRI (mainly Indonesian).

The present Governor, Dr. Johan Henri Ferrier, also served as Prime Minister in 1945.

The late Johan A. Pengel (NPS), another important political figure, was Prime Minister in 1969 when a general strike forced his cabinet to resign, and a new election to be held.

With the exception of three years during which a coalition (the United Front) took over, the NPS had remained in power until the 1969 election. Since unification seemed necessary for political power, a coalition was again

Reminiscent of a small château, the Ministry of General Affairs was once a governor's mansion and is now the Prime Minister's office.

29

launched by leaders of the UHP, the PNP and other groups. When the coalition won the election in 1969, UHP party leader Jagernath Lachmon was appointed *"Cabinet-formateur"* by the governor, a procedure peculiar to the Dutch political system. Lachmon then presented a proposed cabinet to the governor for appointment, with Jules Sedney (PNP) as Prime Minister. As can be seen, selecting a prime minister is an indirect process.

Eddie Bruma, founder-leader of the militant Nationalistic Republic Party, "proclaimed" Surinam a republic in 1963, but this move was unsuccessful. While many citizens feel that Surinam will become independent in the future, there is at present only a limited activity for independence.

From this building, the Ministry of Home Affairs, Surinam's internal matters are regulated.

4. PEOPLE

SURINAM TAKES GREAT PRIDE in its multi-racial society, where many different ethnic groups live together in harmony. The "world in miniature" theme is expressed in the design of her flag, which contains five different colored stars representing the various races, bound together by a band.

A wonderful vitality lies in the diversity of these people—Creoles (Africans), Europeans, Chinese, East Indians, West Indians, and Indonesians—all of whom make distinct contributions to a vibrant nation.

Surinam's rapidly growing population has increased from 70,000 to 420,000 in the past decade. The current rate of population increase is 4 per cent per year. More than 80 per cent of the Surinamese people live in the coastal lowlands, with over two-thirds of them in the capital.

The largest segment of population is made up of Creoles, American descendants of mixed American-Indian and African blood—sometimes a European strain is there as well. Almost equal in number are the Hindustanis from India. Indonesians are third, followed by the Bush Negroes, Europeans, and Chinese. But the descendants of the American Indians (Amerindians) who originally inhabited the area have dwindled to less than 2 per cent of the population.

CREOLES

Over 300,000 Africans were brought to Surinam as slaves. After their emancipation in 1863, many of them left the plantations, and most of their descendants prefer to live in town. Strong believers in education, they are teachers,

Secondary-school students busily at work reflect the varied ethnic backgrounds of the people of Surinam.

Ladies in fanciful Creole costume dance in lively fashion during a folk festival. The Creoles are mainly of African stock with some European admixture, and their traditional clothing is adapted from styles of the 18th century.

This East-Indian Surinamese girl is already wearing the headdress of a grown Hindu woman.

civil service employees, or workers in industry. Many hold high positions in government and the professional world.

The costume introduced to Creole women by modest Moravian missionaries has become a national symbol of Surinam. These attractive *koto-missies* or petticoat ladies of the territory wear long, full, print dresses over starched petticoats, with a bustle in back. The manner in which they tie their head scarves conveys a special mood or message. Certain knots signal love, friendship or trouble. Others say "Hug me tight," or "Wait for me on the corner."

HINDUSTANIS

In general, Hindustanis have been less willing than Creoles to move to other parts of the country. Over 34,000 East Indians were brought to Surinam in the 19th century. Their high birth rate and remarkable success in business has caused a slight rift between Surinam's two major population groups.

These East-Indian people brought with them

their own language, customs, and religion, which many of them still retain. They are thrifty, ambitious, and industrious citizens, who save their money to go into business whenever possible.

INDONESIANS

Still more closely bound by heritage and respect for tradition, the Javanese from Indonesia have been even less changed by Western culture than the Hindustanis. Preferring to live in their own rural communities, these passive, co-operative people make excellent small farmers. Sarong-clad Javanese can be seen barefoot in the mud flats planting their rice seeds by hand.

The Indonesians seem to like Surinam. When importation of contract (indentured) workers stopped, Javanese immigrants continued to come freely to Surinam. Arrivals have recently decreased, since conditions have changed for the better in Indonesia.

EUROPEANS

Most European immigrants were Dutch, but other nations were also represented. Surinam has always had a large, wealthy Jewish community, many of whom came from Portugal, Brazil, or Amsterdam. One of the oldest Sephardic Jewish settlements in the Western Hemisphere was located at Joden Savanne on the Suriname River. Once a prosperous business town, it has long since disappeared, but the cemetery and ruins of the old synagogue can still be seen.

Few Europeans reside in Surinam today. KLM, the Dutch airline, each year carries 16,000 Surinamese to settle in the Netherlands through its half-fare plan, which applies to all Dutch citizens travelling within the Kingdom. But few Dutch fly the other way to emigrate to Surinam. It is this ability and desire to become Dutch residents as much as anything else, which hampers Surinamese efforts to gain independence from the Netherlands.

CHINESE

Major competitors of the Jews, Lebanese, Levantines, and Armenians in small retail businesses are the Chinese. The few thousand Chinese who came to Surinam as plantation workers soon exchanged farm work for town life. Now they own many of the best restaurants and shops. In the cities, Chinese clubs frequently publish their own newspapers and provide health care for their people. They also operate stores in the interior, where they sell to the Amerindians and Bush Negroes.

BUSH NEGROES OR MARRONS

Since the climate and terrain of Surinam are similar to that of Africa, the Bush Negroes, descendants of imported African slaves who ran away, found it easy to retain their ancient

Girls of Chinese origin wear the traditional sheathlike sleeveless dress. The high collars are to cover the backs of their necks. It is an old Chinese custom that still persists, to regard this area of the body as very private.

traditions. Anthropologists are especially interested in studying them since their current way of life is very much like that of 17th-century Africa.

After the blacks made a long series of raids on plantations, the white settlers were forced to make treaties with the Marrons. Bush Negro chieftains still come to the capital to receive tribute money from the Surinam government. The sturdy, self-reliant Bush Negroes look down on most white men and on town Negroes, whom they call *bakra schlaff*, or white man's slaves. The Marrons consider themselves prisoners of war rather than former slaves.

Six Bush Negro tribes inhabit Surinam, the largest of which is the Sarramacca, also known as the Djukas. Each tribe is headed by a *granman*, who presides over the council of elders. The village, in turn, is governed by a village chief and his council, but most power rests with the heads of family groups. Each cluster of huts in a village belongs to a *mbe*, or family group.

Since their major transportation arteries are rivers, streams, and narrow trails, bordered by trees, tangled vines, and undergrowth, most Bush Negro villages are located along river

The Bush Negroes are the descendants of Africans brought to Surinam as slaves in the 17th century. Their ancestors did not remain slaves very long, but took to the woods, where they rebuilt the tribal life they had known in Africa.

Decked with banners, typical dugout canoes of the Bush Negroes take part in a festival. Tourists often have an opportunity to view the fascinating folkways of these sturdy people.

In a Bush Negro village, the thatched roofs of the cottages have eaves that almost touch the ground!

banks, frequently at the head of a rapid, which provides a natural defence.

A typical village contains low, wooden, two-room, A-shaped huts, with palm-thatched roofs. The fronts of many houses are elaborately carved or painted with African designs. The front room is used for living and the back for sleeping. Cooking is sometimes done in a communal shed, with a common storehouse,

community building, council house, and shrine containing religious deities.

If a man has more than one wife, he must provide a home for each and her children. If he can afford it, he also owns a *godo wose* (treasure house) for himself, where he keeps his own personal property.

Small children go naked in the jungle, while older ones wear tiny cloths hung from a cord

These typical Bush Negro structures are built of thatch.

Some Bush Negro houses are built of planks.

Bush Negro boys stand in front of the village store.

A guide waits for tourists as Bush Negro villagers look on.

Bush Negroes in vivid clothing pull a canoe toward the shore of a stream near their village. Great skill is required to pole the canoe through the swirling rapids.

A Bush Negro uses a hefty wooden stick to pound meal.

around their waist. Men wear loin cloths and sometimes throw over one shoulder a toga made from different pieces of colored cloth sewn together like a patchwork quilt.

Women dress in a knee-length, wrap-around skirt, sometimes no more than a towel. On cool evenings, they might wear a stole. Both men and women are fond of jewelry, such as bracelets, necklaces, and brass leg bands. Many wear both a cross and a Star of David as ornaments. Some Bush Negro men and women tattoo intricate scar designs on their skin by rubbing red rice hulls into open cuts.

They live by hunting, fishing, and growing small crops of rice, maize (corn), yams, cassava, and sugar cane. Agriculture is hard work in the jungle since ants and rain quickly deplete the soil. New fields must be continually cleared and fast-growing plants hacked out.

AMERINDIANS

When they fled from the plantations, the ancestors of the Bush Negroes drove native Amerindians from their small settlements on the river banks deeper into the jungle and took over their farms. Unlike the Bush Negroes, the Amerindians are rapidly decreasing in numbers.

The proud expression worn by this Amerindian woman is typical of her race. When the Dutch settlers first came, they recognized the aborigines as free people and let them withdraw to the interior. However, the Dutch record is not so good with the enslaved Africans whom they brought in to work the plantations.

Many of those who remain still live in the jungle very much the same way they did when the first European explorers arrived. Far more at home in the wilderness than in civilized areas, they continue to retreat farther inland as settlers arrive.

At one time, these Indians were better hunters and boatsmen than the Bush Negroes, but the latter seem to have been much more able to adapt. The Indians seem to grow apathetic with the advance of the white man. The women, who do most of the work, however, seem less affected than the men.

The men hunt and fish with traps, rifles, blow-guns, poison darts, bows and arrows. They also carve canoes, benches, and paddles, as well as cut down trees where crops are to be planted. The women do the rest of the work—cooking, nursing, planting, spinning, sewing, harvesting, carrying water and firewood—willingly.

Many Carib women still wear *queyas* (short aprons), heavy strings of beads, and woven cotton bands below the knees and above the ankles. On festive days, they add more beads

Amerindian villagers line up beneath spreading banana leaves to be photographed.

An Amerindian village is landscaped with flowers and banana trees that these descendants of the aborigines have planted.

and perhaps a shawl thrown over one shoulder. Most Indian men wear Western-style shirts and pants, sometimes adding an *olak* (feather head-dress) and necklace made of beetles or animal teeth to celebrate special occasions.

Feasts are given to celebrate a marriage, funeral, new home, or for no reason except that someone feels inclined to entertain and has enough food and drink on hand.

In each hut is a canoe-shaped trough to hold *paiwarie*, an alcoholic beverage drunk by the whole family, as well as clay pots, hollow gourds, baskets, and low wooden benches. From the beams hang many red-dyed hammocks.

Indian huts vary according to the climate. In swampy areas, they are usually built on poles over the water. Many forest dwellings are without walls, while those of the savannah have clay walls to keep out the wind. Most have palm-thatched roofs.

Clusters of forest huts stand in small clearings, walled in by tall trees, where cultivated crops mingle with wild growth.

Each family is ruled by the father, who is influenced greatly by the *peaiman*, or witch doctor. The head man of the tribe organizes hunting and fishing expeditions and settles disputes within the settlement. In each vaguely

Amerindian women have fun welcoming tourists visiting their village.

An Amerindian mother and child display typical hair style and ornamentation—the mother is heavily tattooed, and both wear thick strands of beads.

they had disappeared, but other tribes kept telling about seeing the "strong, fierce giants of men with white skins."

Three expeditions made during the 1960's brought back clues like footprints, pottery, and used camp sites. Finally, in 1968, Christian Indians on a mapping survey discovered the wild Akoedi Indians on the Waremapan Creek near the southeast border of Surinam, and made friends with them.

According to a missionary, Ivan Schoen, the 28 nomadic hunters and gatherers they found were shy but not fierce, well-built but no larger than the average Indian, white-skinned probably because they spent so much time in the jungle shade. They ate fish, meat, honey, and the heart of the wild palm.

Since these Indians had no cultivated fields, the missionaries plan to teach them how to farm so that they can become less nomadic, and

defined district, one Indian is generally recognized as captain.

There is no regular time for sleeping or eating. A pepper pot stew made of meat, rice, okra, peas, beans, and hot red peppers, is kept on the fire all the time, and one dips cassava bread in the stew and eats whenever he feels like it.

Most Indians habitually turn their eyes toward the ground, giving the impression of timidity. This is probably due to the fact that they have trained themselves to repress any sign of emotion when near outsiders.

Wild, nomadic Indians in the southern rain forests are difficult to track down, since the names and locations of their villages constantly change. Stories about a Stone Age tribe of paleface Indians in the interior had grown more vivid each year. Many experts believed

A young Amerindian mother carries her whimpering child in a sling.

how to create their own written language. Five Trio Indians, whose language is similar, were left behind to find out if there was any pattern to the Akoedis' wanderings.

LANGUAGE

While the official language of Surinam is Dutch, a great number of languages are spoken. Many Chinese, Hindustanis, and Indonesians still speak in their native tongues. The Amerindians also use a large variety of native dialects.

The most common form of speech is *taki-taki*, a pidgin language which originated with the Bush Negroes but is spoken and understood by almost all citizens. *Taki-taki* is a mixture of Dutch, French, English, Spanish, Yiddish, Portuguese, and African words. Linguists trace its development to the fact that the slaves came from various African tribes, each of which spoke a different dialect. In order to communicate, they were forced to adopt the language of their various owners.

Not being able to write, they pronounced words exactly as they sounded. For example, *fow* means chicken, *dasnoti* means "that's nothing," *gahdo sabby* means "God understands," and *gran dankee* means "thank you very much." "*Masra wantem-wantem*" is an impatient person, and "*me disee no lobbee*" means "I don't like it." *Bakra* is an African word for white man. The *bigi bakra* is the top white man, and the *bigi missy* is none other than Her Majesty, the Queen of Holland.

Many Indian words also sound like variations of English or Spanish. For instance, *porko* is pig, *supo* soup, and *richi* rice.

Saramacca *tongo* or *deepi taki* is spoken by the Djukas of the interior. Bush Negroes also have a secret language called *odo*, which is impossible for others to understand.

HEALTH

Their eating and drinking habits make Amerindians especially susceptible to disease. Tuberculosis spreads fast because all members of the family eat out of a common pot. They also drink a strong alcoholic beverage made by chewing

This pretty young woman with a basket on her shoulder is a member of an Amerindian family.

cassava roots and spitting them into a container, where the liquid is allowed to ferment.

Surinam's death rate is highest among these people who, in spite of attempts to educate them in proper hygiene, find it difficult to adjust to modern civilization.

Health statistics are high, however, by any tropical standards. Typhus, typhoid, yellow fever, and malaria, all common problems in hot, humid countries, have been brought under control. Venereal disease occurs most frequently in the capital, while yaws is more prevalent in the jungle. Enteric fever and amoebic dysentery are less common in Surinam than in most tropical countries.

In 1949, the Filaria Control Service was organized to combat worms, which are prevalent among people who walk barefoot in the jungle. The Leprosy Control Service has also been successful in isolating that disease.

The Princess Juliana Mission Hospital in the jungle of Surinam District is famous for its

The Moravian Hospital in Paramaribo provides the most up-to-date medical care.

treatment of tropical diseases. Health facilities in Paramaribo include three hospitals.

While many primitive people still turn to the witch doctor for treatment, they are, nevertheless, fascinated by the miraculous skills of medical doctors. If one member of the family gets a pill, every member wants one.

EDUCATION

Considering the many primitive citizens, the 70 per cent literacy rate is higher than might be expected. Education is compulsory up to 12 years of age. The current laws regulating public education and teacher licensing were passed during the early 19th century. In addition to its own system, the government also aids religious-supported schools.

While there are two teacher training colleges, there is still a shortage of teachers, and many receive their education in Holland. Surinam also has a medical school, a law school, and several technical schools. Courses in nursing, forestry, engineering and domestic science become more popular every year.

LIBRARIES AND MUSEUMS

The Surinam Culture Centre and Museum of Ethnology in Paramaribo both contain libraries. The museum, located in Zorp en Hoop (Care

Surinamese youngsters generally are proud of their secondary school, one of many new educational facilities in the territory.

The new university makes the people of Surinam rightfully proud.

and Hope), an impressive new residential section, contains rare books, engravings, native crafts, and historical documents. There are also museums in Fort Zeelandia and Nieuw Amsterdam.

SPORTS AND RECREATION

Surinam's soccer team takes part in Olympic games and World Cup competitions. Over 8,000 people often jam the spacious stadium in Paramaribo to watch important matches. Basketball games are played at the Sports Hall.

In 1963, the government organized the Foundation for the Development of Sports, through which leaders hope to build national spirit and bring the people closer together. A new sports center was built in the capital to train future players and coaches.

Golf, cycling, tennis, swimming, and badminton are also popular. In western Surinam, near the Guyana border, natives seem to enjoy cricket as much as the English do.

Hunters, anglers, and naturalists can now fly to the interior in a short time and stay in comfortable guest houses built and maintained by the government.

ARTS AND CRAFTS

A nation of many races naturally has an abundance of art forms. The Surinam Culture Centre's excellent art school encourages free expression. Native arts and crafts are exhibited at the Museum of Ethnology.

Surinam's Bush Negroes take great pride in their wood carvings. Girls are wooed with works of art, and the boy who carves the most

In the 1968 Olympics, Surinam was represented on the Dutch team by sprinter Eddy Monsels (middle).

43

Hans Lie has recently made the switch from Impressionistic technique to Expressionism. His oil paintings and copper sculptures adorn banks, hotel lobbies, and hospitals.

beautiful drum, paddle or canoe is the one who wins the maiden. Popular motifs are serpents and liana vines.

Both Amerindians and Bush Negroes seem to have instinctive feeling for good design but no conscious technique. Their hand-carved trays, plates, gourds, and ceremonial stools are magnificent.

Amerindian women weave baskets and bake pottery in open kilns. Since they use no potter's wheel, they build a bowl up strip by strip on a flat slab, using only a stick, large leaf, polished stone, and gourd as tools.

The Javanese are famous for not only wood-carving, but also wickerwork and vivid batiks, while Creole, Chinese, and Hindustani artisans make intricate gold and silver jewelry.

Many of Surinam's contemporary artists exhibit their work throughout the world. Painters Nic Loning and Hans Lie both describe their art as expressionistic, while Ab Jongman claims to be a landscape artist who is drawn toward abstraction.

Lie specializes in both painting and copper sculpture, in which he makes strong comments on social problems, such as hunger and poverty. Loning was recently commissioned to design a stamp which would commemorate the 200th anniversary of Kerstens Department Store in Paramaribo. Ab Jongman's appreciation of nature is almost a religion for in it he sees change and erosion, which are symbolic of the temporary nature of life.

FOOD

Rice is the main dish in Surinam, but people are fond of variety and very high seasoning. *Rijsttafel* (rice table), invented by the hearty-eating Dutch colonists in Java, consists of boiled rice and many side dishes of meat, vegetables, seafood, curry, peanuts and various kinds of sauces. Served with fried rice, it is called *nasi goreng*.

The national dish is a thick pea soup made with sausages and potatoes. Other Creole dishes are *pom*, poultry with ground taro roots, and *pastei*, poultry with vegetables.

Popular sweet dishes are *tom*, a heavy pudding made of frou-frou (plantains pounded to a dumpling-like consistency), and *dokun*, a highly seasoned pudding composed of peanuts, raisins, and cassava, served in banana leaves. Also served in this manner are *akansa* cakes made from corn ground with sugar and raisins.

There are numerous good Chinese restaurants in Surinam, and most hotels serve Indian food. Curries are usually made with beef or chicken rather than mutton. Indian tortilla-like cakes, eaten with meat and vegetables, can be bought at snack shops.

RELIGION

No one faith is officially recognized or given financial support by the government. In the Paramaribo vicinity, there are Islamic (Moslem) mosques, Jewish synagogues, Chinese Tao shrines, Hindu and Buddhist temples, a Roman Catholic cathedral, various Protestant churches, and, down one side street, a voodoo shelter.

The first Jews and Moravians arrived in Surinam during the early 17th century. Fleeing from southern Europe and Brazil, the Jews settled south of Paramaribo, where they built Berache Ve Shalom, the first synagogue in the Western world. When Holland took over Surinam, these Sephardic Jews were joined by other Jewish refugees.

The Moravians fled from Central Europe to Surinam, where they built a meeting-house called Herrnhut (The Lord's Care), won many converts, and taught them European trades.

Surinam's East Indians, Chinese, and Indonesians include Moslems, Hindus, and Bud-

This woman doesn't need a shopping cart. In Paramaribo's open-air market, it is a simple matter to bring home enough fresh fruit and vegetables for dinner—just by using one's head!

dhists. Like Christians, the Moslems are also interested in winning converts. Strict Moslems kneel facing Mecca and pray five times a day. They hope to make the pilgrimage to their Holy City sometime in their life.

In comparison with the Moslem religion, Hinduism, which is divided into many sects, is a more complicated system of beliefs and customs. It is a kind of pantheism, which holds that god is present in everything. Surinam's Hindus still worship the gods of their homeland, as well as avatars, manifestations of these gods in nature. Most homes include a small temple with a stone monument and bronze statue. Banners flapping from tall bamboo poles are remnants of the Puja ritual, during which a family offers food to the gods.

Buddhism, which grew out of Hinduism, retained many of its beliefs, such as reincarnation of souls.

Taoists believe that while everything in the world has been designed to move in an orderly and harmonious fashion, man often loses the way by creating his own design. In order to achieve harmony, he should avoid fame, be good to all living things, and return to simplicity by giving himself over to the Great Tao, or Way of Life.

The Roman Catholic cathedral in Paramaribo dates from 1885 and is one of the largest wholly wooden churches in South America.

The domes and minarets of a mosque in Paramaribo remind one that Surinam is the home of many Moslems.

In all these religions, lies, theft, killing, intemperance and other forms of immorality are forbidden.

Many Amerindians and Bush Negroes claim to be Christians, but their worship still retains heavy pagan overtones. While the orderly Dutch have influenced religious rites, many natives are still animists, who believe that there is a soul in all natural things.

Although people are inclined to dismiss natives' stories about *wintis*, witches, or werewolves as superstition, each culture has its own beliefs and rituals which should not be derided.

Surinam natives have many different names for sorcerers—*lukuman*, *wisiman*, and *wintiman*. A *kartaman* tells fortunes with cards, while an Amerindian soothsayer is known as a *peaiman*. Bush Negroes greatly respect the magic powers of Amerindians, since they were the original inhabitants of the land and would be more likely to have control over its earth spirits.

This is not rural India, but rural Surinam. The elegant little mosque serves a congregation of "Hindustani" farmers. Moslems make up 20 per cent of Surinam's population.

46

Stately palms flank the historic Dutch Reformed Church in Paramaribo.

Both good and bad *wintis*, or spectres, haunt the woods and waterways so one must always ask their permission to travel. Furthermore, one should never call the name of a rapid before crossing it, or the water god who lives there might become angry and upset the canoe.

Visitors are advised to duck under the *azang*, arch of palm fronds placed over the entrance of a village to keep out evil spirits. Silk-cotton trees, traditional home of the Earth Mother, often mark the beginning of a Bush Negro settlement. No white man is allowed to enter the magic town of Dahomey, and no Bush Negro will tell you anything about it.

Bush Negroes will, however, talk about the supernatural powers of certain animals, including snakes, monkeys, jaguars, and alligators. Special fertility dances take place whenever someone kills a tapir or manatee.

A good Indian *peaiman* must have the ability to put a spirit into the body of anything he desires—a rock, tree, rapid, bird, insect, fish or reptile.

The *kenaima* and *peaiman* are the two most influential factors in an Indian's life. From the *kenaima* come almost all injuries, misfortunes or illnesses, which the *peaiman* attempts to remedy. To Indians, like Bush Negroes, all objects contain a body and a spirit, which are not easily separated. *Kenaimas* use their powers to separate a spirit from its body and send it to obey certain orders.

In addition to his power over spirits, the *peaiman* also knows how to talk to animals, how to use various healing herbs, how to interpret dreams and visions, and where to find the best game.

In order to become a *peaiman*, an Indian undergoes harsh endurance trials, such as long fasts, wandering alone in the forest. He is also trained to use his voice effectively in the same manner that an opera singer does. He must be

The Moravian Church in Paramaribo is noted for its fan windows.

A fetish guards the entrance to this Bush Negro hut.

able to use strong stimulants and work himself up into a condition of frantic ecstasy.

MUSIC AND DANCE

Music and dance are so closely allied to religion that they can scarcely be separated. Since these are two of the most important elements of pagan worship, they do as much as anything to bind Surinam natives to their past.

Dansi-dansi, social dancing, is a popular pastime of the Surinamese, but *bongo-dansi,* or spirit dancing, to the rhythm of sacred drums, has been discouraged since slave days. It still continues, however, in remote areas.

The sacred drums, made from hollow logs covered with animal hides, are the most important musical instruments used by Bush Negroes. These drums summon the gods, interpret their messages to the people, and send them back when the ritual is finished. Dancers face the drums and dance toward them.

The carved *apinti,* or tenor drum, with its intricate rhythm, calls the sky spirits and ancestor gods, while the *tumao* controls the bush spirits. The long *agida,* or bass drum, played with a strong steady beat, summons the snake deities. A good drummer is said to have strong gods.

Other musical instruments include clay, bone, or bamboo flutes, panpipes, shell horns, rattlers (seed-filled gourds), a *wiri-wiri* (the iron head of a hoe scraped with a metal rod), some form of cymbals like a tambourine, and a wooden box or board beat with a stick.

Bush Negro music is typically African in tone and structure. A soloist is usually accompanied by drums and hand-clapping, with an alternat-

These Surinamese children are performing one of Indonesia's ancient dances. Javanese immigrants have clung to their folkways and traditions.

ing chorus. In dancing and singing, the leader improvises and others follow. Calypso (*kawina*) songs and dance are popular among the Surinamese, too.

One of the most violent dances, with a frenzied tempo that often brings on trances, is the Bush Negro *kromanti*, which glorifies their brave African ancestors.

To prepare for the ritual fire dance, a witch doctor first paints the dancers' bodies, empties a bottle of rum or beer as offering to the gods, then arranges an *obia* house with twigs, a doll, a green bow-tie, a bottle of rum, and several small pieces of cloth.

Rhythm is furnished by drums similar to African tom-toms, and the dancers are also accompanied by weird, high-pitched singing. During the performance, dancers walk across, roll, and jump on hot coals and broken glass. They rub themselves with burning branches, pour boiling water over themselves, and chew pieces of broken glass and burning wood. They also stick red-hot blades into their flesh. When the hot machetes touch their skin, there is no sign of a burn.

Some believe that the fire dancers coat their skins with anesthetic liquid, while others think the feats are made possible through self-hypnosis. Whatever the explanation, it is an unforgettable sight.

At their *piwarie* feasts, Amerindians march around the liquor trough chanting, keeping step and waving their instruments in time to a certain rhythm. Suddenly, they cry out, drink, and move outdoors to dance.

Steps differ with tribes, some slow and stately, others fast. In one dance, men and women stand in lines facing each other. At other times, they link arms and strut around together, bending backward, forward and from side to side.

Some dances imitate animals. In the jaguar dance, one man plays the animal, creeping around and carrying off the others one by one until he is left alone.

Each dance is ended by a loud roar, the signal for more drinking. Any person who has too much to drink and starts trouble, is sewn up in his hammock. When the dancers are exhausted, they retire and sleep, then wake up and begin the feast again. This sometimes goes on for days, until all the food and drink is gone.

At the other end of the spectrum is the delicate, stylized Balinese dance, accompanied by an ensemble, which one can often see performed by sarong-clothed Javanese on Saturday night in town and in the countryside on a Sunday afternoon. The orchestra is an assortment of bronze and wooden instruments, plus something resembling a xylophone.

The Javanese *rejog* is an ancient dance drama that tells the legend of a king who loses his betrothed to another, but wins her back by dressing in disguise and riding a hobby horse, to defeat his enemies. A monkey dance depicts an incident from the Hindu Ramayana legend.

Another way in which the Javanese pass down legends, traditions and philosophy is through a puppet play with an ancient theme. The story action is portrayed by shadows cast on a screen.

The Bellevue Theatre (now a cinema house) in Paramaribo is 100 years old.

At one of Surinam's many festivals, this young Surinamese wears the carnival dress of his Javanese ancestors.

CONTEMPORARY MUSIC AND DANCE

At Surinam's art centre, the most popular class is dance. One teacher specializes in African choreography, while others teach Oriental dances. Classical ballet is enjoyed in Surinam, but local artists are creating many new dance forms which better express the character of their country.

In addition to art and dance courses, the Culture Centre also contains a school of music. The Surinamese have excellent singing voices and enjoy being a part of choral groups.

The National Philharmonic Orchestra, made up of talented volunteer members, gives several concerts each year and is especially interested in promoting the work of native composers.

HOLIDAYS AND FESTIVALS

Also closely connected with religious rites are Surinam's various festivals. There always seems to be a feast going on somewhere in Surinam, where even birthdays are celebrated with great fervor. Since Oriental religious holidays are governed by the lunar calendar, their dates vary each year.

On New Year's Day, Hindustanis sprinkle each other with tinted water, while the Chinese celebrate with dragons, firecrackers, and future prophecies.

Hindu and Chinese wedding ceremonies are both elaborate affairs. After a three-hour Hindu wedding, usually at night, each guest expresses his wishes to the couple by dipping his hand in white rice and ginger and imprinting it on the side of the house.

The Hindu festival of Lord Krishna lasts for nine days, while the Feast of Ramlila is highlighted by a pageant telling the life story of Ram. During the Feast of Lights, tiny lamps outline

New Year's Day is observed in Paramaribo as celebrators in elaborate costumes parade through the streets.

Food, drink, and burning incense play an important part in every Hindu wedding ceremony. The liquid used is not water, but amrit—*the "holy water" of the Hindu faith. The small wedding party sits shoeless on the ceremonial floor and forms a circle, the symbol of man's life cycle, around a pot of flame. The fire stands for life itself, and toward the end of the rite the priest makes the flame leap up while the bride and groom with their attendants march slowly around it seven times, each circle bringing another blessing to the newly wed pair.*

each house, fence and path. The Hindu *pandit* (learned man) and his helpers beg and make meat offerings at a palm-decorated shrine to celebrate the reincarnation of Vishnu.

While the Islamic Fast of Ramadan is not as strictly observed in Surinam as it is in other Moslem communities, Sekaton commemorating Mohammed's birthday, is a festive occasion.

To celebrate a Tadjah festival, a procession of veiled women in colored saris and turbanned men in white, playing flutes and drums, will carry small mosques made of bamboo and colored paper through the streets. This feast extols Mohammed's two grandsons who were killed in a battle for succession of the caliphate.

People of all races take part in the *komjejari* (fair) and National Sports Festival held at the end of August. Freedom Day (July 1) is a national holiday on which various ethnic groups parade in costume, while *koto-missies* dress in full regalia at Creole dancing parties.

The Surinamese celebrate the Queen's birthday as well as the usual Christian and Jewish holidays. At Easter, they present a special version of the Passion Play, which relates the life of Christ to the various races of Surinam.

Both Amerindians and Bush Negroes hold many festive rites, including the celebration of each new season, with presents for the gods. During these ceremonies, Indians wear ornate costumes with ribbons, tassels and beads. The men also wear necklaces of beetles and boars' teeth, with elaborate headdresses of bright bird feathers.

FOLKLORE

Surinam's varied assortment of people are especially fond of proverbs, riddles and legends, many of which are connected with plant and animal life.

While funeral wakes are a popular time for story-telling, almost every afternoon, small groups gather and listen to tales. The usual heroes are Makuki, the smart monkey, Koni-Koni, the cunning rabbit, and a clever spider

51

This is a shoe shop in Noorderkerkstraat, typical of old Paramaribo, with its gables, dormer window, and galleries.

called Anansi, who is able to outwit everyone with his skilful manoeuvering.

Like Creoles and Bush Negroes, the Indians, as they lie in their hammocks or squat around the fire at night, listen to stories told by the *peaiman*, head man, or an old woman. Many of these stories relate to ancient tribal wars. Others are about a great flood, fire, or creation of the world.

The recurrence of these legends in slightly different form all over the world is not surprising since all primitive people have experienced floods or fires, and tend also to speculate about how people came into existence.

The Arawaks believe that a supreme spirit broke off twigs and bark from a silk-cotton tree and scattered them all around him. Some fell in the water and became fish, some became birds, some beasts, and some human beings.

The Caribs, who believe that their brave men will live after death in happy islands with Arawaks as their slaves, tell about one of their ancestors who lived in the sky. This fearless hunter followed a bird for days before he finally hit it with his arrow—the bird fell into a deep pit. When the hunter looked down and saw daylight, he climbed down a rope to clean the dirty kingdom, and came back with venison. The other sky-dwellers liked it so much that they also went below, but one fat woman got stuck in the hole and could not be moved.

The Caribs also have their version of the Great Flood. The animal, the agouti, discovered the magic tree from which all cultivated plants are derived, but kept it a secret. After his fat paunch aroused suspicion, the god Makunaima had him watched. When he and his twin brother, Manape, found the magic tree, they decided to pull it down even though the agouti warned them that a large volume of water would spill out and submerge the earth. When the floods came, seeds of this miraculous tree were spread all over the world.

5. ECONOMY

SURINAM'S ECONOMIC CONDITION is closely related to the history of the territory, which was under the rule of colonial powers for over 400 years. First signs of a planned economic policy came with the appointment of a development commission in 1909. Several decades passed, however, before this plan could begin to offset the centuries of colonial administration.

First Surinam had a one-crop sugar economy, then came gold, cacao, coffee, rice, balata, and finally the bauxite and alumina industry. After World War II, a development fund was introduced. The Ten Year Development Plan went into effect officially in January, 1955. The following Five Year Plan had as its goal an annual 7 per cent increase in Gross National Product. The current Gross National Product has exceeded this goal by achieving a rate of 9.5 per cent growth. The per capita GNP is $450, which is well above the South American level.

A favorable balance of trade was first realized in 1966, followed by a serious inflation threat in 1967, due to profiteering and inadequate marketing facilities. In 1967, however, there was a $4,000,000 surplus, compared to $2,200,000 the year before, caused mainly by increased refining of bauxite within the country.

Surinam's development plans emphasize full exploitation of the territory's natural resources and the encouragement of industry to generate capital and improve the general standard of living. The country has a wide variety of resources, but terrain, climate, and dense vegetation have impeded their development.

MINERALS

Annual shipment of over 4,000,000 tons of bauxite in either the raw or processed state (aluminium) make this the country's Number

A modern fork-lift truck moves slabs of processed aluminium that is ready for shipment. Bauxite, the principal ore from which aluminium is extracted, is one of Surinam's chief natural resources.

Huge power shovels scoop up bauxite from an open mine.

One export, accounting for 78 per cent of the total. In fact, two-thirds of the ore used in the United States comes from Surinam. And another huge deposit, just discovered in the west of the territory, has still to be mined.

Surinam expects to process more of the bauxite within its borders as time goes on. In line with this, the only integrated aluminium plant in the world was constructed, where the ore is both processed and smelted in just one operation.

The most exciting new development in the mineral sphere, however, is the discovery of oil on the coast north of Paramaribo. The government has signed an agreement with Royal Dutch Shell to drill for crude oil. Petroleum Surinam Corporation, a French subsidiary, holds the rights for offshore exploration.

Iron ore has been discovered but will be mined only when further exploration proves that deposits are sufficient to make it financially rewarding. More efficient methods of processing the ore within the country are also being studied.

Manganese is just below the level necessary to guarantee profitable exploitation. Gold, once a large source of income, is now of little importance. Deposits of tin, mica, nickel, cobalt, lithium, kyanite, tantalite, columbite, beryllium, platinum, and diamonds of jewel quality have also been detected.

ELECTRIC POWER

Since manufacturing requires large amounts of power, the country is now concentrating on

Bauxite is washed and dried in this plant before the alumina is refined from it. (Aluminium smelting is the third stage.)

Clouds of dust arise as bauxite is loaded aboard a cargo ship.

an increase of hydro-electric power, with hopes that it can encourage further industrialization.

Surinam's many swift rivers afford excellent possibilities for the generation of energy. The powerhouse of the new Affobakka Dam has an electric potential of 180,000 kw.

Proposals to dam up the waters of the Courantijne River near Cow Falls met with serious obstacles since the reservoir to be formed would inundate lands lying within Guyana territory. Dams are projected near the Kabelebo Airstrip in the west and on the Avanavero Rocks.

AGRICULTURE

Even though agriculture is the second largest industry in Surinam, and over half of the people still live on farms, there are few large plantations left. Actually, less than 1 per cent of the land is under cultivation.

After bauxite, the next biggest export is rice, which is grown mainly in the coastal lowlands.

The Brokopondo Dam on the Suriname River near Affobakka was built to provide hydro-electric power for smelting aluminium extracted from Surinam's bauxite-rich soil. The recent discovery of huge bauxite deposits in southwestern Surinam is expected to bring hydro-electric power to that part of the country, too.

As Surinam seeks to develop its hydro-electric power resources, more dams and power projects are in the planning stage. This is an architect's conception of a dam soon to be built.

Decline of sugar production was a blessing in disguise since it called attention to the fact that Surinam should not depend on one crop alone but aim, instead, for diversification.

In addition to rice, other big crops are sugar, coffee, cocoa, corn, citrus, peanuts, bananas, and coconuts. But the country still imports more food than it exports.

WAGENINGEN PROJECT

In the 1950's, a Dutch foundation hired men to hack through jungle near the Guyana border and reclaim 18,000 acres for cultivation. This land was to become the largest mechanized rice-growing project in the world.

Rice seeds are planted by aircraft, and combine harvesters reap the crop. The cut rice is brought in by boat to be milled, then sent up the Courantijne to Nieuw Nickerie on the coast, where it is loaded onto freighters for export.

The project is divided into several sections. On one polder, small farms are run by owners who have access to research, mechanical, and selling facilities. Experts from all over the world come to Wageningen to study its techniques. Only two crops are planted annually now, but scientists hope to develop a strain which can be harvested three times a year.

LIVESTOCK

Cattle-raising is done mostly by farmers on small plots, but an attempt at large-scale ranching is also being made by a United States investor on the savannah near the Brazilian

Rice is processed in this plant at Wageningen on the Nickerie River.

Bananas are an important crop in Surinam. The trees are really gigantic perennial herbs, which wither to the ground and die there after bearing their huge clusters of fruit.

border. The government is also promoting dairy farming and poultry raising.

FORESTRY

Timber, especially plywood, is Surinam's third largest export. Bruynzeel Plywood's huge forest concession, started in 1947, provides a factory in Paramaribo with over 60,000 tons of fancy timber each year. It turns out panelling, parquet flooring, concrete plywood, particle board, and prefabricated parts for houses.

Aerial photography has made it possible to map the forests, which cover 75 per cent of the territory, according to types and density. The government sponsors many projects. Heavily wooded areas have been opened by road and drainage, while young trees have been planted in cleared areas. The Carib pine, imported from British Honduras, makes excellent raw material for the manufacture of paper products.

The large brown pods of the cacao tree look like long, thin coconuts. Inside the pods are seeds from which cocoa, cocoa butter, and chocolate are made. The cacao tree is native to South America.

57

The wild bully tree provides an elastic gum called "balata" which is used as a substitute for rubber. To tap the gum, workers called "bleeders" make grooves in the bark. This allows the milky juice to flow downwards to the base, where it is collected in pails. It is dried on zinc boards, then made into mats, and sold to village traders.

Huge logs float down the river on rafts on their way to the lumber mill.

Some of the most valuable wood in the world is processed in this factory, which started from a tiny office in Rotterdam, Holland. The Bruynzeel Plywood Company has made timbering the second largest industry in Surinam.

New housing of the type seen here figures prominently in Surinam's development plans. Many of these housing projects will accommodate Surinam's rapidly growing corps of industrial workers.

FISHING

Since fishermen changed from seine netting to trawling, shrimping has become a major industry. The number of shrimp vessels doubled to 150 in 1969. Boats now have facilities on board to process and freeze the shrimp while at sea.

INDUSTRY

The discovery of oil and increased supply of electric power should help to encourage industry, which is now limited to bauxite smelting, wood products, rice mills, sugar refineries, distilleries, breweries, coconut oil plants, cigarette manufacturing, small clothing factories, paper-bag and box making, printing plants, a Venetian blind company, and a synthetic detergent factory.

COMMUNICATIONS

International Telephone & Telegraph Company (ITT) signed an agreement with the government to modernize and extend the country's communication service. ITT's assembly plant in Surinam is also used to ship parts to Europe. The 300-foot-high radio tower at Wageningen is one of its spectacular achievements.

Surinam has five radio stations (three in Paramaribo), one television station, four daily newspapers, and six weekly periodicals.

TRANSPORTATION

Climate and terrain have hampered the improvement of transportation facilities. Surinam's rivers are navigable only by shallow draft boats. Internal transportation is mainly by boat, car,

This construction of a radio tower in Vailliant Plein is a step in the project to modernize Surinam's communications system. Surinam has enlisted the aid of ITT in carrying out this project.

The International Telephone and Telegraph Corporation (ITT) has constructed a new plant at Morgenstond. (See also the ITT undertaking on page 59.)

truck, plane, and small buses with names like "OK, LET'S GO" or "NO TIME TO LOSE."

Alcoa Aluminum and the Royal Netherlands Steamship Company operate ships between Surinam ports, Holland, and the United States. Surinam Steamship Company also provides service to Caribbean ports.

The only railway in the country, from the capital to the gold mines about 100 miles south, once ran through the coastal region, savannah, and rain forest. Much of the track has been submerged by Lake Van Blommestein, however, and will not be replaced.

The opening up of Surinam's interior by highway will be dependent on a desire to develop natural resources. The northern east-west road through the coastal plain opened up farming areas, while the central east-west road connects major bauxite areas and opens up the forest belt.

An east-west road north of the mining region will join the central highway, connecting important dam sites with the Kabelebo, Coppename and Suriname Rivers. Two north-south roads are also projected, which will open up eastern and western production areas.

In a scene that recalls the Netherlands, cyclists pedal across a drawbridge in Paramaribo.

The terrace of the fashionable Torarica Hotel in Paramaribo overlooks the Suriname River.

PORT FACILITIES

The scuttling of a German freighter in 1940 made it easier to construct Paramaribo's new $100,000,000 deep-water port, which centralizes warehousing and customs facilities and caters to over 26,000 ships a year. A deep area carved out around the wrecked vessel by strong currents formed the base for the new port. The work was financed mainly by European Common Market funds.

TOURISM

A recent international survey revealed that tourism in Surinam is expected to increase five-fold in the next decade. At the moment, 32.5 per cent of Surinam's 6,220 yearly tourists come from the United States and 23.4 are sight-seers from the Netherlands. Jungle tours are expected to remain the big attraction, but visitors from many diversified nations will swell the ranks of the curious, adding more than the already significant $2,000,000 to Surinam's economy. As a result, government officials are planning to build new hotels and enlarge those already existing. Modern guest houses have been constructed in the interior at Operation Grasshopper airstrips. Hunters, fishermen, explorers, and photographers are encouraged to penetrate formerly inaccessible jungle areas by plane.

AIRLINES

The interior is also being opened up by Operation Grasshopper, which is busily clearing airstrips at important locations. Each new strip serves as a base for further exploration.

Zanderij, the airport for Paramaribo, has changed in the last 30 years from a short narrow runway on the savannah to one of the most modern airports in northern South America, used by several international airlines, including KLM, BWIA, Air France and Pan American.

Surinam still needs more direct connections with other South American lands, especially their cities. And Surinam Airlines, formed in 1962 as an internal service, is already looking to other Latin American countries. It currently flies to Guyana, Trinidad, Curaçao, and French Guiana as part of an airline pool. It also owns a crop-spraying company, which plays an important role in local farming.

FINANCES

Surinam's currency has never been devalued. The official rate of exchange is now 57 guilders or florins per United States dollar. The Centrale Bank, which issues banknotes and mints coins, doubled its output within 10 years. Since two Dutch banks recently merged to gain control of 80 per cent of total

The modern-looking Surinaamsche Bank provides a striking contrast with Paramaribo's colonial architecture.

deposits, United States banking firms have shown great interest in investing in this field.

The Ten Year Economic Development Plan provided for extensive capital investment in mining, forestry, industry, education, agriculture, and public utilities. The new Five Year Plan involves a $7,000,000 investment with 50 per cent a gift from Holland and 40 per cent a low-interest loan.

Surinam continues to receive aid not only from Holland but also from the European Common Market, the United Nations and the United States AID program. Its aid-per-capita ratio is one of the highest in the world.

FOREIGN INVESTMENT

Surinam offers generous incentives to pros-

pective foreign investors, including a 5- to 10-year tax exemption for certain industries. The government encourages ownership of private property and stimulates free enterprise. In addition to many untapped natural resources and hydro-electric potential, its assets include a stable currency and democratic tradition, as well as a large pool of energetic workers. Major liabilities are a small domestic market and undeveloped distribution channels.

Upon his retirement from business, Willem Bruynzeel, the timber man, persuaded the Dutch Government to boost private enterprise in Surinam by covering large financial risks. The Foundation for the Promotion of Investments in Surinam, located in The Hague,

The Hollandsche Bank Unie has its offices in this unusual-shaped building in Paramaribo.

The Centrale Bank of Surinam (right) issues the country's banknotes and mints its coins.

encourages businessmen to reinvest profits within the country, thereby helping to accelerate its development.

The annual Surinam Trade Fair has grown so rapidly since 1955 that it is now a major display point in South America for ideas and merchandise, attracting firms from as far away as England, Taiwan, Denmark, Indonesia, and Puerto Rico.

FOREIGN TRADE

Surinam's increasing prosperity is reflected by the fact that its export growth rate doubled within two years.

Imports (45 per cent from the U.S.) are mostly machinery, chemicals, food and food products, motor vehicles, and petroleum products. Other major import-export partners are Canada and the European Common Market countries. In 1969, a new preferential tariff schedule for EEC members went into effect, which encouraged this trade even more.

PUBLIC WELFARE

Surinam has a far-reaching welfare system, with social security and pension plans covering workers in government and private business. Employees have the protection of the International Labor Organization, which regulates pensions, benefits, compensation, safety inspections, and arbitration.

TRADE UNIONS

A teachers' strike, followed by sympathetic unions, led to a large general strike in 1969.

Little boys everywhere are fascinated by construction. These youngsters are watching a pile driver at work in Vailliant Plein.

Unwilling to meet union demands, the Pengel cabinet resigned and was replaced by an interim government made up of leading men in trade, industry, and labor. Realizing their influence in government, the unions, since then, have stepped up organization. Even though many skilled workers are being lost to Holland, unemployment of potential employees is still about 10 per cent.

"Hindustani" women plant rice in a paddy. The descendants of Hindu and Moslem immigrants from India are known locally as "Hindustanis."